ADVENTURES WITH ZOOBY™

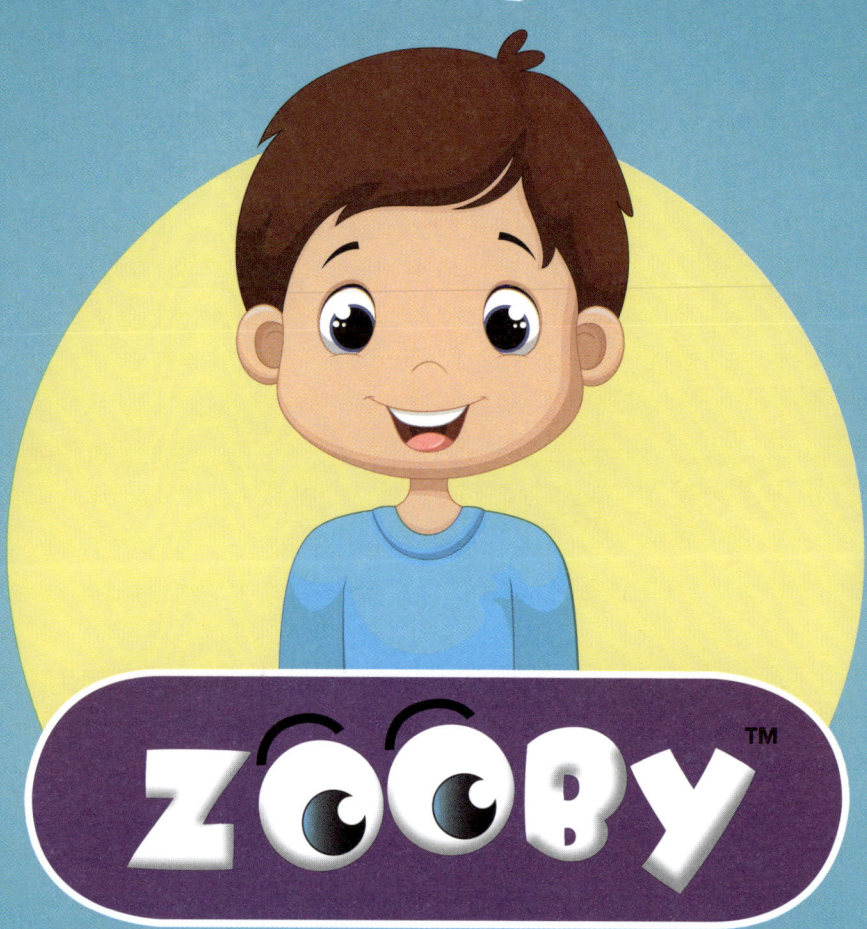

Max goes to the dentist!

Written & Created by Michelle Bain
Contributions by Zooby Dental

DISCLAIMER. This book provides general information about dental health. This information is not intended to be used for the diagnosis or treatment of a health problem or as a substitute for consulting a licensed health professional. Consult with a qualified physician, dentist or health care practitioner to discuss specific individual health needs and to professionally address dental health or medical concerns.

MEET MAX!

Max is getting ready to leave for the dentist soon. This is his first time going to a dentist's office.

MAX WAITS IN THE WAITING ROOM

at the dentist's office. There are so many exciting things to do in the waiting room.

"HI, MAX! COME ON BACK."

The first friendly face Max meets belongs to Holly. Holly is the hygienist.

FIRST UP,

Max gets to choose which toothbrush Holly will use to clean his teeth.

MAX LOVES TIGERS,

so he chooses to have Talon the Tiger clean his teeth!

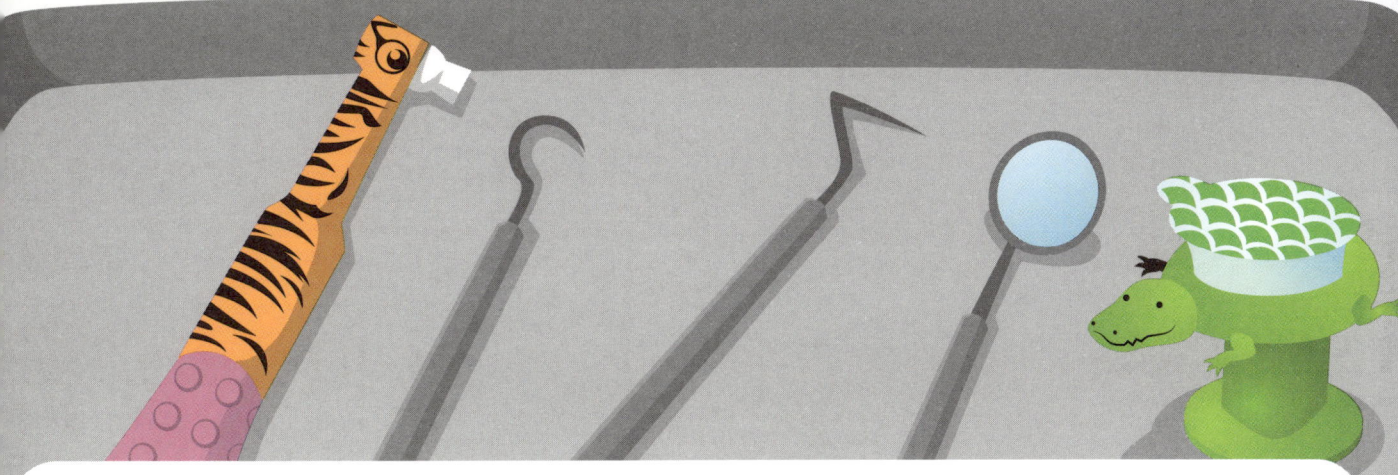

Next, Holly will use a special toothpaste to clean Max's teeth. She gives Max lots of flavors to choose from. Which will it be?

- **HAPPY HIPPO CAKE**
- **SPEARMINT SAFARI** 
- **GROWLIN' GRRRAPE** 
- **GATOR GUM** 
- **CHOCOLATE CHOW** 
- **TURTLE MELON** 

Happy Hippo Cake it is! Yum!

WEARING TALON THE TIGER MAKES MAX ROAR!

"OKAY, MAX.

We'll use Talon and the Happy Hippo Cake toothpaste you picked to clean your teeth," says Holly.
She cleans the fronts,
she cleans the backs,
she cleans the tops,
and she even cleans between Max's teeth.

THEN HOLLY USES A SPECIAL

vitamin on Max's teeth to clean and protect them. This will guard his teeth from sugar bugs.

NOW IT'S DR. KAREN'S

turn to see Max. "Who is this brave little tiger in my chair?" she asks Max.

Dr. Karen looks at Max's teeth to make sure they are healthy.

"IT'S IMPORTANT TO BRUSH

your teeth the right way," Dr. Karen tells Max. "Brush all the way around each tooth. Front, back and top. Brush for two minutes at least twice a day. Don't forget to floss once a day, too! Doing that will really make those tiger teeth sparkle!

Your teeth look great, Max! We will see you in six months for your next visit!" says Dr. Karen.

HOLLY GIVES MAX A BAG.

In it are a new toothbrush, toothpaste and floss for cleaning his teeth at home.

NOW MAX'S TEETH ARE CLEAN AND HEALTHY.

He thanks Dr. Karen, Holly and all of the Zooby animals for such a fun time!

MAX'S SMILE

is brighter than ever! And he roars to prove it!

YOUR MOUTH

You start losing teeth when you are about six years old.

As a kid you have 20 teeth but once you an adult you have 32.

PALATE

UVULA (you-view-la)

TONGUE

CANINE TEETH
The four pointy teeth in the corners of your mouth.

WISDOM TEETH
The four teeth in the back of your mouth that grow in around age 17 - 21.

YOUR AMAZING TOOTH

DENTIN
The bony layer under the enamel.

ENAMEL
The hard outer layer that protects your teeth.

NERVES
Let you feel hot and cold foods through your teeth.

PULP
The soft inner part of the tooth.

WONDERFUL GUMS

GUMS ARE THE PINK FLESHY PARTS AROUND YOUR TEETH.

ONLY 2/3 OF A TOOTH IS VISIBLE. THE REST IS UNDER YOUR GUMS.

YOUR GUMS SHOULDN'T BLEED WHEN YOU BRUSH OR FLOSS. IF THEY DO, ASK YOUR PARENTS ABOUT SEEING A DENTIST.

3 STEPS TO HAPPY TEETH!

- BRUSH TEETH ALL OVER FOR TWO MINUTES TWICE A DAY.

- FLOSS ONCE A DAY.

- ASK AN ADULT TO HELP YOU USE MOUTHWASH ONCE A DAY.

© 2017 Pixie Stuff, L.L.C. All rights reserved. All materials are protected by the United States and international copyright law. No part of this publication may be reproduced, distributed, displayed, stored in a retrieval system, or transmitted in any form or by any means, electronic, mechanical, photocopying, recording or otherwise, without prior written permission of Pixie Stuff, L.L.C. You may not alter or remove any trademark, copyright or other notice.

The Zooby characters are © 2016 Young Dental Manufacturing I, LLC, and are used with permission. All rights reserved. ZOOBY and related logo are trademarks of Young Dental Manufacturing I, LLC, and are used with permission. © Young Dental Manufacturing I, LLC.

PIXIE STUFF PUBLISHING, HIRED INK, COMPOSE CREATE CURATE and related logos are trademarks or registered trademarks of Pixie Stuff, L.L.C.

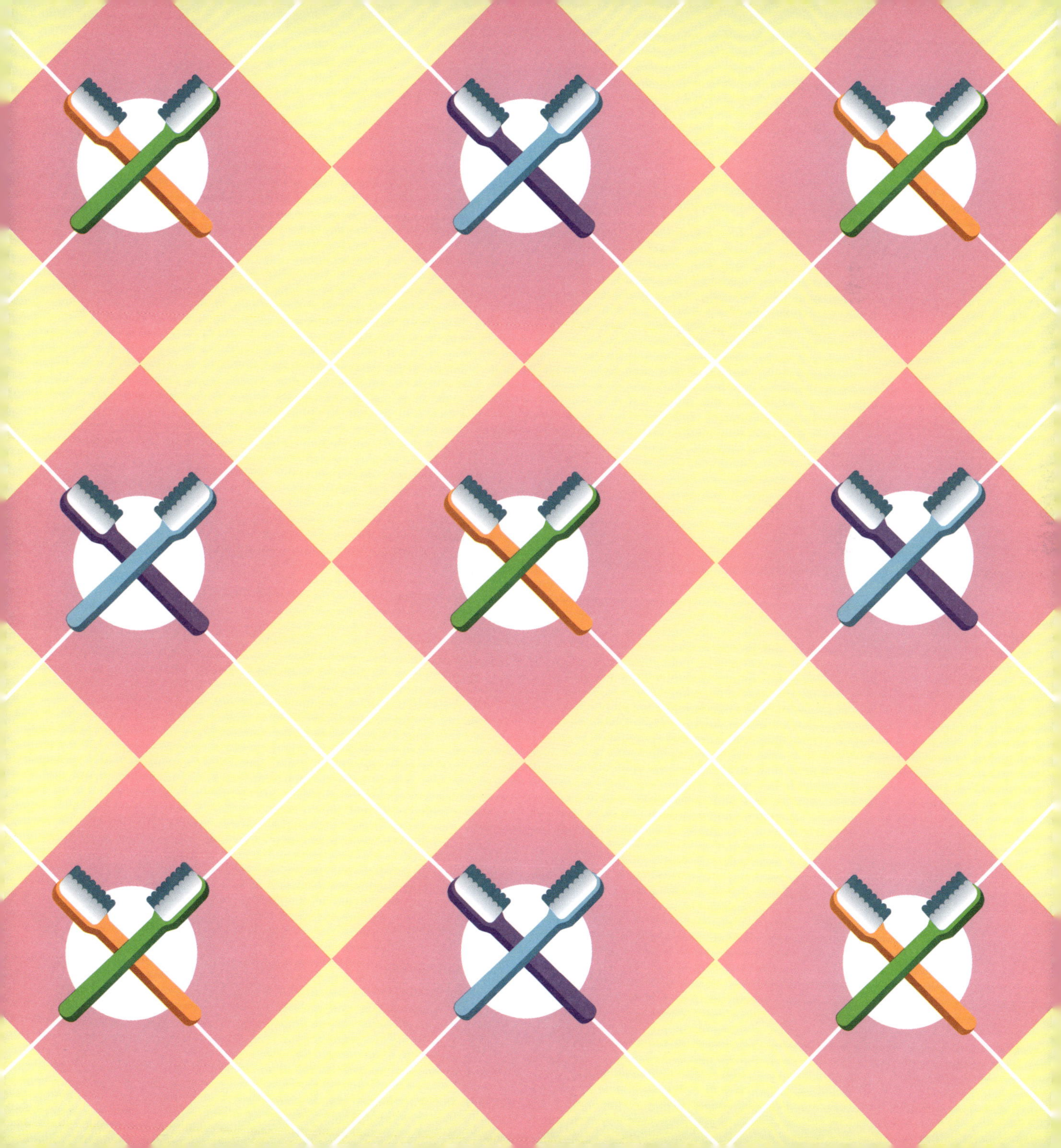

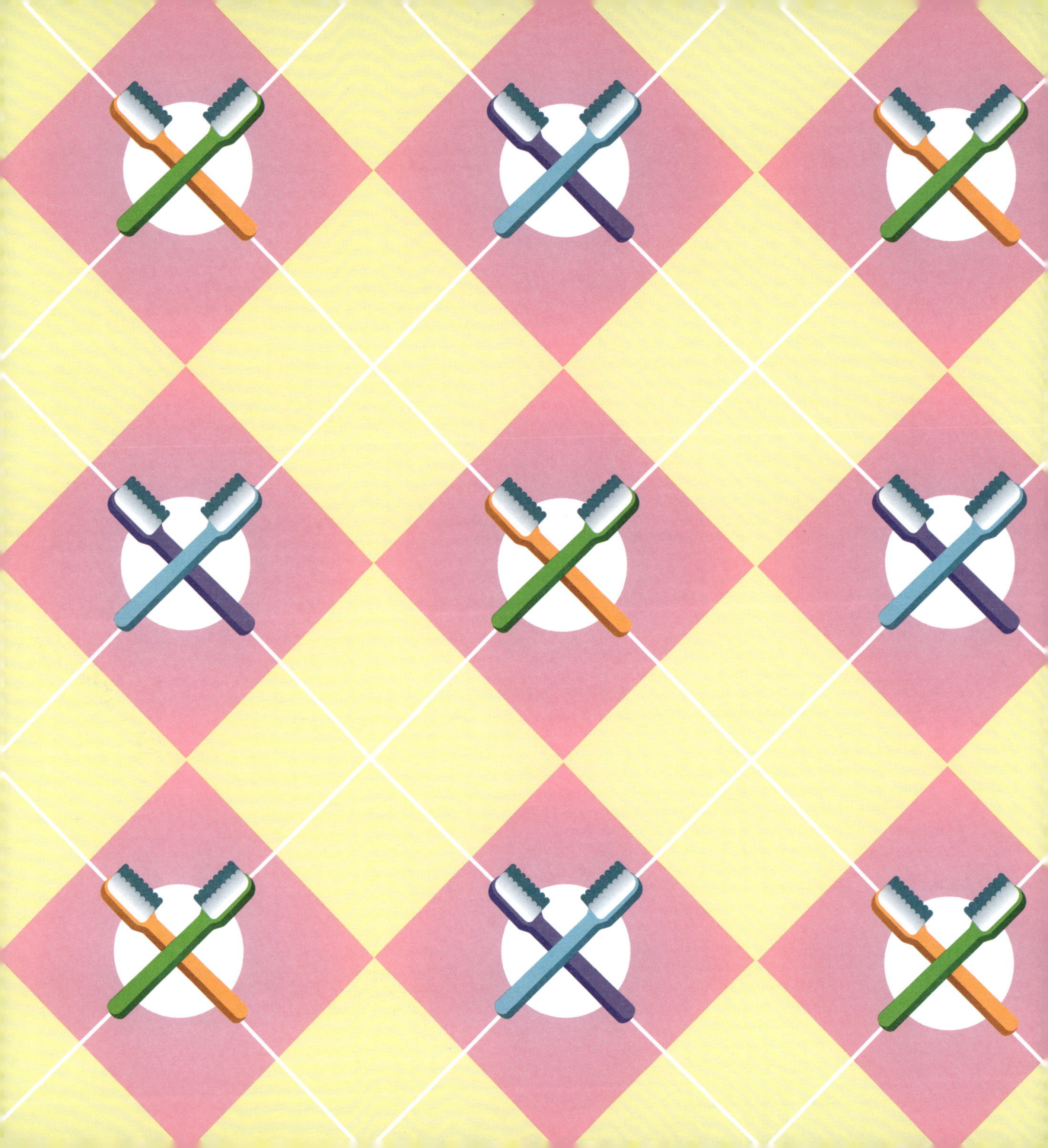